FOREWORD

"Frontiers of America" dramatizes some of the explorations and discoveries of real pioneers in simple, uncluttered text. America's spirit of adventure is seen in these early people who faced dangers and hardship blazing trails, pioneering new water routes, becoming Western heroes as well as legends, and building log forts and houses as they settled in the wilderness.

Although today's explorers and adventurers face different frontiers, the drive and spirit of these early pioneers in America's past still serve as an inspiration.

ABOUT THE AUTHOR

During her years as a teacher and reading consultant in elementary schools, Mrs. McCall developed a strong interest in the people whose pioneering spirit built our nation. When she turned to writing as a full-time occupation, this interest was the basis for much of her work. She is the author of many books and articles for children and adults, and co-author of elementary school social studies textbooks.

Frontiers of America

EXPLORERS IN

A NEW WORLD

By Edith McCall   Pictures by Robert Borja

 CHILDRENS PRESS, CHICAGO

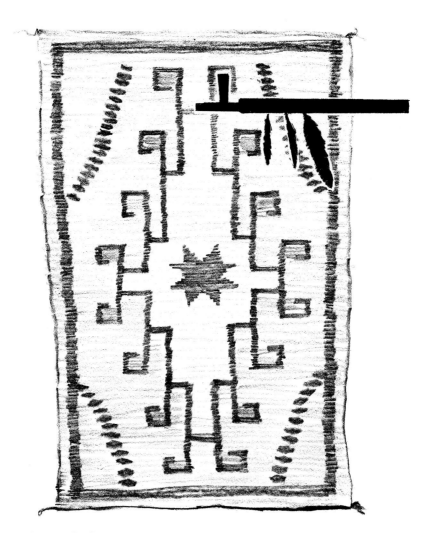

Library of Congress Cataloging in
Publication Data
McCall, Edith S
    Explorers in a new world
    1.   America—Disc. & Explor.—Juvenile
fiction   2.   U.S. Exploring expeditions—
Juvenile fiction.   I.   Title.
PZ7.M1229.Ex   60-6675
ISBN 0-516-03318-2

Cover photograph courtesy
of the National Archives

New 1980 Edition
Copyright© 1960 by Regensteiner
Publishing Enterprises, Inc.
All rights reserved. Published
simultaneously in Canada.
Printed in the United States of America.
6 7 8 9 10 11 R 93 92 91 90

CONTENTS

WESTWARD TO A NEW WORLD

Christopher Columbus was disappointed.

"I can sail west to China and the Indies," he had told the Queen of Spain. "If I find any unknown islands, I shall claim them for Spain. Then, when I have marked the way to the rich islands of the Indies and to the great cities of China, the Spanish trading ships can go back and forth easily."

He showed the queen a map of how he believed the world to be. It had one large continent of Europe, Asia and Africa together, with one ocean around it. There were many islands in the ocean.

"The earth is round, like a ball," he told the queen. "Therefore, ships going in any direction can get back to land. But to go north is to go into the cold lands and icy seas. Marco Polo found the way over the land, eastward. But you know how long the journey is, and now enemies are blocking the way."

Columbus' finger went next from Spain, on his map, southward along the African coast. "Not long ago, a ship went from Portugal south to the end of

Africa. But it is a very long journey. Now see how easy it should be to sail west to China." His finger went across the small mapped ocean, coming quickly to the shores all the European countries wanted to reach.

The queen had nodded and then set about raising money to buy ships for Columbus. He sailed westward as planned. When he landed on an island southeast of North America, he thought he was on one of the islands he expected to find near China. He called the people he saw *Indians,* because he believed the island to be one of the group called the *Indies.*

For ten years, Columbus had gone on trying to find the lands with which Spain wanted to trade. He was sure that China could not be far away. He died in 1506, a disappointed man, sad that he had not found the way through all those annoying islands to China. Even then, he had no idea of how large North and South America were.

Columbus had not heard about the journeys of the men of northern Europe, the Norsemen. They could have told him that there was a large body of land far to the north of where his ships sailed. In their little open boats, the Norsemen had traveled westward many

years earlier. They had found Iceland and Greenland, and then had gone west to Newfoundland, near the mouth of the St. Lawrence River.

Right after Columbus made his famous journeys, more Spanish ships sailed west. They nosed into bays and river mouths along the shores of Central America, the northern part of South America, and the part of North America that is now Mexico. The explorers finally decided that all this land was part of a "new world," which none of them had known. But they were not pleased to have found it, for it was in their way. It blocked their sea path to China. As the ships nosed into the river mouths, it was their masters' hope that the river would be a passageway through the land. Then their ships could sail on to China.

The explorers talked to the Indians as best they could in sign language until they learned to understand a little of each other's languages.

"Yes, there are great rivers," the Indians told the white men. "We know not where they go, but they reach far toward the setting sun. Stories have come to us of a great sea into which the sun falls each night."

The explorers, since they could not find their way

through the land, thought perhaps there might be something worth finding in the New World. To them that meant gold and jewels, spices and silks. The Indians seemed to understand when they asked about the yellow gold.

They said, "In the land of the setting sun, there are great cities. There they have the yellow gold."

The Spaniards' imaginations built cities whose streets were paved with gold, and where wealth was theirs for the taking. From then on, they looked for two things—the way to China, and the golden cities.

There were many who came to the New World. There was Amerigo Vespucci, who talked so much of what he found that the land was named for him, "America." There was Ponce de Leon, who had been one of Columbus' men. While De Leon was governor of Puerto Rico, he heard the Indians talking of a rich land across the sea to the north.

"There is gold there, and something better," they told De Leon. "There is a river whose waters make an old man young again."

Ponce de Leon's mirror told him that such a "Fountain of Youth" would do more for him than any

amount of gold. He paid for ships himself, and sailed northward. The land he found, on Palm Sunday, in April, 1513, had blooming trees and wild flowers.

Florida! He named it in honor of Easter, or *Pascua Florida*. He searched, but found no gold and no Fountain of Youth. He went back to Puerto Rico. When he returned in 1521, strong winds and stormy seas tossed his ships about. Before he could land, unfriendly Indians fought from the shore. De Leon lay dead on board his ship.

In the meantime, many other places had been explored. England had sent John Cabot, who landed far north of the Spanish findings, at Newfoundland, where the Norsemen had been. Spanish ships had followed the west coast of Florida around the Gulf of Mexico and all the way down to South America. Balboa had crossed the narrow neck of land now called the Isthmus of Panama. On a September day in 1513, he had seen the great Pacific Ocean. Others had gone to Peru in northwestern South America. There they really found rich cities, those of the Inca Indians.

About the same time that Ponce de Leon was killed, Magellan reached the Philippine Islands, sailing west, and was killed there. His ships went all the way around the world, and the earth's size was known.

That same year, a Spaniard named Cortez was riding his great horse into the cities of the Aztec Indians in Mexico. The Indians had never seen horses before. The big Spanish horses frightened them. At first they thought the horse and rider were one great monster. And when the guns the Spanish carried struck them down from far away, they were terrified. Cortez and his men moved on and took all of Mexico.

Except for Ponce de Leon's trip to Florida, no attention had been paid to the land that was to become the United States of America. No one had any idea how large that great mass of land was.

Then, in 1527, some Spaniards were shipwrecked off what is now Texas. They were made slaves by the Indians. One of the Spaniards, Cabeza De Vaca, was allowed to go free in order to go on trips to get things the Indians wanted. He became a trader, bringing sea shells to Indians who lived far from the sea, and taking back hides, flint and red dye to the Indians who lived near the ocean.

Little by little, De Vaca worked his way westward.

Nine years after the shipwreck, he reached the Gulf of California. He was the first white man to have crossed North America.

De Vaca told true stories of what he had seen and many tales that he made up. He enjoyed seeing the eyes of his listeners widen with excitement. He told his stories in Mexico, and then he went back to Spain and told them there. In both places, listeners were sure there was a land north of Mexico called Cibola, and in Cibola there were seven cities of gold.

INDIA

NORTH

AMERICA

JAPAN

CUBA

SOUTH AMERICA

FROM AN
EARLY MAP

SEARCH FOR SEVEN CITIES

A tall black, dressed in the skins and feathers of an Indian, and a small Spaniard in the brown robe of a monk stood before the governor of part of Mexico.

The governor, Francisco Coronado, had an eager look in his eyes as he spoke. "De Vaca spoke of great cities he saw, cities that sparkled from afar with the gold in their walls. Did you, too, see those cities, Estavan?"

The black nodded. "Yes, I was with De Vaca when he saw them."

"I, too, saw them from afar," said the monk, Friar Marcos.

Coronado was pleased. "They must be the Seven Cities of Cibola," he said. Every Spaniard had heard of the wonderful cities. No one knew exactly where Cibola was, or who had first told of its seven cities. Coronado pictured the cities as having walls and streets of gold, set with rubies and emeralds and sapphires. Inside the buildings, there would be chests of riches waiting for him and his men to take.

His fist struck the table. He would go, and these two would go with him to show the way! But to do that, he must have the help of Mendoza, the man who had taken Cortez' place as Viceroy of New Spain.

"You two will take another journey," he said. "I must have more reports for Mendoza."

A worried look crossed the monk's face. "Sire, there are great dangers . . . . ."

"Yes, yes. I shall send soldiers with you." Coronado's voice pushed aside all the dangers as if this were but a trip to the next village.

Estavan and Friar Marcos, with a few Indian guides and some soldiers, were soon on their way to Cibola, which was supposed to be in the north, near the country where De Vaca had traveled. Estavan and Friar Marcos had been among the shipwrecked men who had wandered in the valley of the Rio Grande.

When they reached a place in what is now southern Arizona, Friar Marcos called the men together.

"From here there are many ways we could go," he said. "Some should go one way, and some another. There is not time for all of us to go all directions, so I shall stay here to wait for your reports. If you find a city, send a messenger back with a wooden cross. Send a small cross if the place is small. If you have good news, send a cross as long as your two hands."

The men set out in small groups. Estavan led the way for one of the groups. He enjoyed going into the Indian villages. He dressed himself in skins decorated with feathers. Around his neck he wore a necklace of chunks of turquoise, given to him by Indians he had visited. As he drew near a village, he always sent a messenger ahead to say a great medicine man was coming.

Then he would go toward the village, bounding and leaping and crying out. The Indians, seeing the black giant, would bow down before him and then offer him everything they had. To a man who had lived most of his life as a slave to the white man, this was a great joy.

Estavan and the handful of men with him reached the edge of a cliff. They looked down into the open valley. There, sparkling in the sunshine, was a city whose walls were the yellow of the gold for which the Spaniards hungered.

"One of the Seven Cities!" Estavan cried.

Surely those buildings, reaching high into the air,

had walls of golden bricks. The gates to the city were golden, too. The blue specks on the doors must be sapphires. Estavan jumped and kicked his heels together in the air.

"Go now!" he said to one of the Indian guides. He gave him a gourd to which two bells and a red feather and a white one were attached. This sign was usually understood to mean that a medicine man was coming.

Then he called out, "Wood for a cross!"

The Indian who carried the sack in which the sticks of wood were carried took out two which would make a cross as long as his two hands.

Estavan pushed them to the ground. "Larger! This is a city like none we have ever seen!"

A cross was made of the longest sticks that could be found.

The messenger started on his way back to Friar Marcos. Then Estavan, leaping and jumping, flew down the hill towards the city. Straight toward the gates he went, shouting and singing at the top of his great voice. The other men followed behind him, slowly.

Estavan stepped inside the gates. The other men,

still high on the hillside, watched as he entered. They saw him hold out his hands for the gifts he expected. But instead of bowing and holding out gifts, the Indians in the city seized the big man and took him inside a building. The watching men waited. Estavan did not come out. There was no more sound of his great voice echoing through the valley.

They scrambled back up the cliff and hurried away. They stopped only to catch their breath until they reached the place where they had left Friar Marcos. The little man's eyes showed his fear as he listened to the tale they told. But he dared not go back to Coronado and Mendoza without having seen the city with his own eyes.

He made his way cautiously as far as the cliff's edge. There he looked down and saw the great city for himself. He did not know that the hot, dry air added glitter and color to what he saw. Perhaps he really believed that the city in which Estavan had disappeared was built of gold and sapphires. The adobe walls of the pueblo were of yellow clay with straw and bits of sparkly mica in them. The blue color came from chunks of turquoise in the doors. Even the yellow corn, piled high, may have been taken for gold.

Friar Marcos, after one look, turned quickly and headed back to New Spain as soon as his men had gathered. The report he gave Mendoza and Coronado set their eyes afire. Soon Coronado, with a large band of soldiers and Friar Marcos to lead the way, was off to conquer the Seven Cities of Cibola.

Mendoza thought their supplies should be carried by ship, traveling up the Gulf of California. No one knew just how far north the cities were, and they thought the ship probably could go near them. Three months after Coronado and his three hundred men in shining armor set out, three ships set sail. They were under the command of a man named Alarcon.

Alarcon found the mouth of the Colorado River at the north end of the gulf. No ship had ever gone into the river before, and there was no one who could guide the men. Alarcon found that the river's current was too strong for his sailing ships, and for fifteen days the crew struggled along the banks, pulling the ships with ropes. They reached the place where Yuma, Arizona, is now, where the Gila River joins the Colorado. Indians were camped there.

"How far to the great cities?" Alarcon asked. "Have you seen an army of men on horses?"

The Indians could tell Alarcon only that they had heard of Estavan, and that the city where he had disappeared could be reached from a trail that ran to the Gila. Alarcon turned his ships up the Gila, leaving messages for Coronado now and then.

In the meantime, Coronado's army had marched to the northeast, taking each Indian village on the way. They came at last to the city where Estavan had disappeared. Indians at work in the fields near the village saw Friar Marcos. They had heard of the man in the brown robe who had been with Estavan. They cried out angrily.

Coronado was not a gentle man. He was cruel, and the yells of the Indians brought out his anger. He waved his sword and spurred his horse forward. The army of men on their great horses charged into the city.

The Indians fought as well as they could, but there was not much they could do. They knocked Coronado off his horse and were about to kill him when he was rescued by his men. Coronado, as soon as he was on his feet again, slashed his sword this way and that in great anger. Into the little rooms of the pueblo he and his men went, killing everyone near. Coronado's anger grew almost into madness when he failed to find gold or jewels. At last, disgusted and discouraged, he and his men rode from the ruined city.

All through the southwestern part of what is now the United States, Coronado and his army rode, seeking the other fabled cities. They found no riches.

One group of men were sent westward to explore. They found something greater than any golden city, although they were only angered at having their way blocked. The earth suddenly ended, it seemed, and dropped down into an unreachable valley where the Colorado River flowed. They had found the Grand Canyon.

Another group, going southeastward, reached a river bank where Alarcon had been. Alarcon had carved into a great tree: "Alarcon reached this point; there are letters at the foot of the tree."

The men dug up the letters, only to learn that Alarcon had headed back for New Spain. There were no supplies, and Coronado must go home or starve.

Wearily, the army turned to the south. The dream of the "Seven Cities of Cibola" was gone forever. Coronado was disappointed in the land he had found. He could not know of the great civilization that would grow someday in the land he had mapped.

RIVER
IN THE
WILDERNESS

Slowly the wind filled out the sails of the nine ships. Like a flock of white doves, they moved steadily to the northwest, leaving the harbor of Havana, Cuba, behind them.

It was the same year that Estavan met his death many miles to the west. De Vaca's stories had sent Hernando de Soto, the man who led this expedition, in search of the seven cities, too. De Soto, like Estavan, was to give his life in the search.

The winds grew quiet when the ships were well out to sea. The hundreds of soldiers on board the ships grew restless, anxious to reach the shores of Florida and start on their great adventure. From the holds of the ships came the grunts and squeals of hogs and the whinnies of horses, just as eager to reach land. De Soto had brought with him hogs to give meat to his men, and more than two hundred horses for his soldiers.

At last the winds stirred again, and the ships moved on to the place where Tampa, Florida, is now. The men began the march to the north. The officers and lancers of the company of soldiers rode horseback, banners flying and armor shining. After them marched 400 foot soldiers and 100 slaves, carrying the packs of goods. Last of all, driven along by some of the slaves, came the herd of hogs.

Soon the report came to DeSoto from a scout who had ridden ahead. "Indian settlement not far away."

"Does it look like a city of wealth?" De Soto asked.

The scout shook his head. "No, Governor. It is a little camp of huts. But there is a chief among them who may know where the wealth is hidden."

"Get him," ordered De Soto. "Bring him to me."

So began the plan De Soto used all through his travels. The chief was kidnapped and held to keep the braves from fighting. When De Soto was sure there was nothing more he wanted from a village, he put ankle irons and chains on as many braves as he thought he could use as slaves. After he had left the village, the chief was allowed to go back. The chief of the next village took his place.

There was little the Indians could do. The great charging horses frightened them. They could not understand the "sticks that killed." De Soto's men robbed their villages all through Florida and as far north as North Carolina.

"Where are the cities of gold?" De Soto asked at each place.

"Not here! We have no gold! The cities are far away," the Indians told him. When the stories were of cities to the west, he at last turned that way, crossing the Blue Ridge Mountains. As he moved along, now and then De Soto invited a chief and some of his braves to a feast of roast pork. The Indians liked the new meat so well that often they tried to steal the hogs. Sometimes the hogs escaped into the wilderness, too, and from that time onward the wild hog came to be common through what would be southeastern United States.

The stories led De Soto and his men southward almost to the Gulf of Mexico. They came to a large Indian village about where Mobile, Alabama, is now. The village had log walls around it. When the gates were opened, De Soto's slaves slipped inside, carrying most of the soldiers' supplies on their backs.

A fierce battle began. All day and far into the night, the fighting went on. When it was over, almost three thousand Indians lay dead and the city was burned to the ground. As soon as repairs had been made, De Soto hurried his tired men northward again, away from the Gulf of Mexico and a chance to return to Cuba.

At each village, De Soto asked again about the rich cities De Vaca had told about. Each time, the answer was, "The gold is in the land of the setting sun, beyond the Great River that flows to the sea."

De Soto remembered the dreamed-of way to sail ships through North America to the Pacific Ocean and on to China. From that time on, he wanted to find two things—the riches of the seven cities and the passage to the western sea.

At last, in the spring of 1541, they reached the Mississippi River, not far from where Memphis, Tennessee, is now. De Soto climbed to the edge of a bluff. There below lay the widest river he had ever seen.

"The Great River to the Sea!" he said, and his heart jumped at the thought that he had found a waterway through America. He must follow the river to the north to learn how far it was to the Pacific Ocean.

"But first we have to cross the river so that we can follow the trails to the cities of the west," he thought.

Soon his men were cutting down trees to make big rafts.

When they had made the crossing, they went north along the river as far as land that is now in Missouri. They drew near to a great Indian village, where the chief's house was built on top of a mound. Around it were the houses in which lived his many wives and children.

The chief sent men to meet the Spaniards.

"We had word of your coming, men with white skin," they told De Soto. "Our chief bids you, their leader, come under the shelter of his roof."

De Soto did not want to walk into a trap. "Tell your chief that I thank him, but I must stay with my people," he said. Then he added, "Tell him also that we shall come to call with gifts for him."

The next day De Soto took gifts from one of the chests his slaves carried and went to the chief's lodge. The two leaders talked together in sign language.

De Soto carried a small mirror with him. "I am a child of the sun," he told the Indian chief. "I cannot die. Look into this magic I hold in my hand. You will see that a face exactly like mine is there." De Soto held

the mirror carefully so that his face and not the chief's would be reflected.

"That is the face of the spirit who tells me all. There are no secrets he will not tell me," De Soto said.

The chief nodded. This man who rode on a great beast that did his bidding must indeed be a "child of the sun." Arrows would not pierce the hard, shining coat he wore. He had men who carried sticks that could kill.

On Sunday, the Spaniards met for a church service. Several priests had come with them from Spain. The chief and his braves watched the white men praying to their God.

A few days later, the chief sent for De Soto.

"Oh, man of great magic," he said, "we are in need of your help. For many, many days, no rain has fallen. Our corn dries on the stalk before it has grown full. We pray to our gods for rain, but no rain falls. Your God has given you so much that He must be greater than ours. We ask you to pray to your God to send us rain."

De Soto agreed to do this. He had his men cut a great cross from a pine tree. They set it up in the Indian village, with a mound of dirt about it to hold it in place. The priests put on the best of the robes they had with them. As the Spaniards knelt, the Indians stood in silence watching.

That night the moon disappeared behind clouds. Thunder rolled and lightning flashed. The wind rushed through the dry cornfields. Then, with a rush, the rain came.

The next day, De Soto and his men marched onward, loaded with gifts from the grateful chief. Their wanderings took them westward and south and back again to the Mississippi. But always it was the same. The cities of gold turned out to be only ordinary Indian villages, with perhaps a bit of copper or lead instead of gold or silver.

After a year of such wandering, De Soto talked one night with his trusted friend, Luis de Moscoso.

"I am very tired, Luis. We have traveled many miles and found nothing. The river to the sea grows smaller to the north, the Indians say. Winter will come again and we have little to eat. Our clothes are in rags, and many of our men have died. I, too, feel the hand of death upon me."

"Oh, no, Governor," De Moscoso said. "Rest a while and you will grow stronger."

But De Soto shook his head. "I am tired, my friend, and sick at heart as well as in my body. When I am gone, lead my men back to New Spain in whatever way you can."

It was May, 1542, when De Soto died. His men buried him at night, outside the walls of an Indian village near the Mississippi River. They did not want the Indians to know that the "child of the sun," the man who "could not die" was gone forever.

"He is away," they told the Indians. But they saw the Indians looking curiously at the fresh earth on De Soto's grave.

"They will dig him up," Moscoso said. "We can't let them do that."

That night, when all was dark, the Spaniards silently dug up the body of their leader. They carried it to the edge of the Mississippi River. There they unwrapped the skins they had put about the body and loaded them with stone before rewrapping the body.

Without a word, two men lifted the body into a canoe. A third took his place at the back of the boat and paddled them out to the middle of the river.

The men rolled the heavy bundle over the canoe's

edge. De Soto sank to rest at the bottom of the river he had discovered.

Moscoso led the men on more wanderings to try to find their way to New Spain. At last they came back to the Mississippi River. There they built seven small ships, in the woods near the river's edge. The ankle irons were taken off the Indian prisoners and they were set free. The irons, stirrups, spurs and any other bits of metal they could find were melted down to make nails and anchors for the ships.

The tired men took new courage and strength at the thought of leaving the country which had brought them only trouble. They worked hard to fit out the ships. Pitch from pine trees and fiber from plants were used to make them watertight.

A flood came when the boats were almost finished. The Mississippi rose over its banks and floated the boat out into deep water. A few more trees were cut to make masts. Skins, shirts, worn blankets—anything that could catch the wind — were sewed together into sails.

The once proud army went on board their patch-work ships. There were 332 left of the 600 who had

come. Only 40 horses were left of the more than 200. Eighteen were killed for meat for the men, and 22 loaded onto canoes. The sails were opened, and the anchors raised.

But the troubles were not ended. The Indians saw the men who had seemed so strong slipping away. They opened fire. The canoes slowed the escape, and the horses were taken ashore. There was not time to kill them all and some escaped. All the way down the river, the ships were targets for angry red men.

De Soto was gone, but his mark was left on the land that was to become the United States. From the horses which escaped from the Spaniards grew the bands of wild horses of the west. The Indians overcame their fear of the animals and learned to use them as the white man had done, and a new way of life opened to them. The hog, too, became an animal of America.

But most of all, the mystery of a broad section of land and the greatest of North American rivers was cleared away forever.

NEW LANDS FOR FRANCE

About the time that De Vaca was telling tales of the cities of gold, another man sighted piles of ice on a northern shore.

Jacques Cartier, French seaman for more than twenty years, looked at the rocky shore ahead.

"We're too early to go into the bays," he said to the ship's mate. "Look at the ice piled up near the shore."

Cartier had sailed across the sea from France that year of 1534 with two ships and sixty men, for France had joined Spain in an interest in the New World. Many other ships had come that way before him, for French fishermen liked to work off the shore of Newfoundland. But unlike the fishermen, Cartier had come to try to find a passage through North America to the sea that led to China.

"We'll fish until the ice breaks," he decided. The men put the ship's small boats into the water. When they had six barrels of fish salted down, Cartier decided it was time to head into the bays.

They sailed south around Newfoundland and then

west through the strait named for John Cabot who had sailed there thirty-three years earlier. They nosed their ship past Prince Edward Island and northward once more. One morning they saw a wide arm of water reaching westward into the land.

"This could be it," Cartier said. "We shall sail into this bay." It was late July by then, and even the northern country must have been getting warm, for they named the bay *Chaleur,* which means "warmth" in French.

They went on shore. The men cut a tall straight tree and of its trunk they formed a great cross.

Cartier scratched letters onto a board. "Long live the King of France," he wrote, and nailed the board to the cross. After the men had set the cross firmly into the ground, they sailed on to the west.

But by late summer he knew that this was not the passage through to the Pacific Ocean. The weather was growing stormy, and it was time to get back to France. Cartier kidnapped two Indians and sailed back across the Atlantic.

In France, he took the two Indians to show them to the king.

"These men are from a land to the west of the fishing banks," he told the king. "There are arms of water reaching far into the land. The natives say that one of them goes to a great sea."

The king was interested. "Go on," he said.

Cartier said, "Your Majesty, perhaps I could find a northwest passage through the new land to reach the China Sea! Will you give me the ships and men I need?"

The king knew how much such a passage would help France. He decided to help Cartier. The next spring, Cartier sailed again. This time, guided by the Indians, he sailed into the mouth of the St. Lawrence River. Slowly they moved up the river, exploring the near-by land as they went. The leaves were just beginning to turn the bright colors of autumn when they reached the place where Quebec is now.

High on the bluff was an Indian village. Cartier climbed up to meet the chief, Donnaconna. With his Indians to help him, he talked to the chief.

"Where does the great river come from?" Cartier asked.

Donnaconna said, "No one knows. But there are

great seas to the west. Many days' journey up the river, past the rocks and the rushing water, there is another great river. It comes down from the northwest to meet this river."

Cartier's lips pulled tight and his eyes gleamed. Could this be the northwest passage he was seeking?

"I shall see that river myself!" he said.

Donnaconna heard the excitement in Cartier's voice and saw the light in his eyes. Perhaps this man from faraway, with his strange clothes and the long knife in his belt, meant no good to the Indians. Did he want to take the red man's land? Perhaps it would be better if he did not find the river.

"You would not like it there," the chief told Cartier. "The waters are full of rocks, and devils wait there to crash the canoes against them."

But Cartier made plans to go up the river. Donnaconna decided to try something stronger than talk. One day, Cartier saw a strange sight. He was on the deck of his ship where it was tied below the Indian village. Coming toward him in a canoe were three howling, dancing creatures.

As the canoe drew nearer, the creatures almost

overturned their boat in their wild movements. Cartier saw that they wore skins of black and white dogs, and they had horns on their heads over blackened faces. They screamed something as they passed the ship.

"What did they say?" Cartier asked his Indians.

"They say the god of the boiling waters is angry that the white man comes."

Cartier laughed. "We'll show them," he said. He had his men load the twelve cannons of his ships and point them at the wooded shore across from Donnaconna's village. At a signal, all the guns were fired at once.

The boom and the roar was something the Indians had never heard. Their frightened cries echoed across the water. In a moment, not an Indian was in sight.

Cartier set sail soon after. His ships went up the St. Lawrence as far as Lake St. Peter. There he left them because the river ahead was too rough for the large ships. He and a few of his men went on up the St. Lawrence in the small boats they carried on the ships.

All along the way, Indians hurried to the riverbanks to see the strange man who wore a hat with a big curled feather, and whose belted coat had lace at the cuffs. They stared at his white face, with its little pointed beard and flowing mustache.

One day a sailor pointed ahead and called, "Look, Sire! The river divides!"

Cartier's eyes turned quickly to see the northwest passage for which he had been looking so long. There it was, joining the St. Lawrence at the end of an island just ahead to the left. To the right, a short way in from the banks of the two rivers, a mountain rose. On top of it, Cartier could see a large Indian village.

The people were hurrying down to meet the boats.

"They are happy to see you," his Indians told Cartier. "See the dance they are doing? It is a dance of joy."

Cartier watched as the Indians formed three great circles, one of men, one of women and the third of children. They danced a long time. Then the chief invited Cartier and his men to a feast.

The next day, Cartier climbed the mountain. He wanted to see as much of the new river as he could. The leaves were beginning to fall already, and he dared not follow the river now. But he would come back. Surely he was looking now at the Northwest Passage.

He named the mountain Mount Royal, from which the city of Montreal, which grew there later, took its name. Then he returned to the river. Winter came, and in the spring Cartier went back to France to report on his findings.

The king was no longer as interested in the Northwest Passage as he had been. His country was having trouble with its next door neighbor, Spain. He was disappointed that Cartier had neither found gold nor sailed all the way to China. There was little money for more trips.

But Cartier used his own money to go back again. This time the Indians had become worried about what the man from over the sea wanted in their land. They gave him trouble, and he could go only a short way up the Ottawa River before cold weather came. Again he had to go back home. He may have made a fourth trip, with no better luck. Then he sailed no more.

But the young sailors on the docks, where the aging explorer came almost every day, heard his stories of the St. Lawrence valley and the Northwest Passage he had not been able to follow. His dream of a way to China lived on even after Jacques Cartier was gone.

CANOE TRIP TO BATTLE

"This must be the mountain and the meeting of the rivers of which Jacques Cartier wrote," said Samuel Champlain. He and the leader of a new French expedition stood on the shores where the Indians had danced a welcome to Cartier sixty years before. Now the Indian village was gone from the mountain, and the only sounds were of the waters and the birds.

The two men climbed the mountain and looked as far up the Ottawa River as their eyes could see. Champlain felt Cartier's old dream of the Northwest Passage rising within him as he imagined what lay beyond the horizon.

As Cartier had been forced to do, the leader of this expedition turned about, planning to come back later. But he became ill and died. Samuel Champlain, whose work it was to draw the maps and write the reports of what was seen, decided that he *must* follow that northwest river, the Ottawa, to learn if it led to the western sea. The old hope for a trade route to China had not been forgotten.

Five years later, in 1608, Champlain was back in Canada. He reached the place where Donnaconna's village once had stood. Part of Champlain's work was to start a settlement which could be used as a fur-trading center. He looked at the fine rise of land where once the Indian village had been.

"This is the best place I have seen for the colony," he said. Soon his men were busy cutting down the nut trees which had overgrown the land. They used the logs to build three two-story houses and a large storehouse. They built protecting walls and a little balcony that connected the second story of each building with the others. Soon the flag of France was flying over the little fort. The city of Quebec was born.

Then Champlain could begin to think of the second part of his work, the part that interested him most. He wanted to get back to the Ottawa River to follow it. But he knew that he would need the help of the Indians to do that safely, so he set about making friends among the near-by tribes, the Algonquins and the Hurons.

The Indians thought the guns that Champlain and

his men carried were wonderful. War would be easy with those!

"Will you help us when we go to fight our enemies, the Iroquois?" the Indians asked Champlain. The Iroquois, enemies of all the Canadian tribes, lived farther south, where New York state is now.

Champlain thought over the question. Going on trips to fight the Iroquois would slow down his own exploration of the Ottawa River. However, it might be worth it to get the friendship of his Indian neighbors.

"Yes," he said. "We will help you fight your enemy."

A war party gathered. But the braves wanted to see the white man's strange buildings before they went to fight. They came into the fort and built their campfires in the open square. They looked at the wonderful things the white men had brought from over the Sea of Salt. They ran about on the little balcony. But their greatest joy was when Champlain fired the cannons. They howled with excitement at every echoing boom.

After several days, they were ready to push off in their fleet of canoes to go to war. Champlain and a

dozen of his men got into their boat. It was called a *shallop,* and had small sails as well as oars. All the boats headed southwest, up the St. Lawrence.

The shallop could go faster than the canoes, and the Indians thought it would be nice to have sails to do the work of their arms as they paddled trying to keep up. All the boats went through Lake St. Peter. Soon afterward they came to the mouth of the Richelieu River, which flowed into the St. Lawrence from the south.

As the first canoes turned up the Richelieu, Indians in other canoes yelled, "Not here! We do not want to go that way!"

Then began an argument among the one hundred twenty-five Indians. It ended with more than half of them going home. Champlain was quite sure that they had not really wanted to go to war. His shallop and twenty-four canoes, carrying fifty-seven Indians, turned up the Richelieu.

Fifty miles up the river, Champlain learned why the Indians used lightweight birchbark canoes. His shallop could not go into the shallow waters, and he sent it back to Quebec with ten of his men. He and two of his men took places in the canoes.

"I believe we would do well to make canoes for ourselves," Champlain said. Later, when he saw how the Indians could carry a canoe easily when going from one river to another, he saw that this was the best kind of small boat for the country. The French word *portage* came to be used as a name for places where the canoes were carried.

The Indians were disappointed at losing ten men, each of whom carried a gun. But they went on toward the enemy's home country. As they reached Iroquois ground, they began to be more careful, stacking brush around their camp at night.

They came to a peaceful lake. To this day it has Champlain's name, for he was the first white man known to have seen it.

At the southern end of Lake Champlain, they drew near the battle grounds. They came upon a band of over two hundred Iroquois. The two Indian forces met each other at the close of day. It would soon be too dark to fight, so they spent the night yelling at each other. The Iroquois built themselves a brush stockade. The Canadians stayed in their boats.

At dawn, Champlain and the Canadians ran ashore

and through the woods to the stockade. Some of the Iroquois came out to meet them.

Thirty feet from the Iroquois, Champlain and his two men stopped. They aimed their guns and fired at the oncoming enemy. Three men, two of them chiefs, fell to the ground. The rest of the Iroquois stopped short, not understanding what had happened.

So surprised were they at the strange stick that spat out hard balls that killed and at the queer looking men with their enemies that they forgot to shoot their arrows. The Canadian Indians sent their arrows after the shots, and the Iroquois turned and ran.

Champlain's Indian friends shrieked with joy. Never before had they seen the strong, fierce Iroquois turn and run from them. After hours of dancing, they began the return trip to the St. Lawrence River.

Champlain had won their friendship forever. The day would come when the Indians would save him from great trouble.

SEARCH FOR THE NORTHWEST PASSAGE

Samuel Champlain spent the next years tending to the business of fur trading. He had little time to explore, for he had to make several trips to France.

Then, at last, in the spring of 1613, came his chance to look for the Northwest Passage. He hurried to the place where the Ottawa met the St. Lawrence. On one of his trips to Paris, he had met a young man named Vignau. Vignau claimed to have gone up the Ottawa River, and Champlain brought him along as a guide.

Vignau had told Champlain an interesting story in Paris. "At the end of the Ottawa River," Vignau had said, "I saw an awful sight! Oh, the sea was there, all right. But on the beach was the wreck of an English ship, and the bones of eighty sailors. The Indians had scalped them. The only white man left alive was an English boy the Indians held captive."

"You swear to that?" Champlain asked. If this man were telling the truth, the English ship must have come to the Northwest Passage from another direction. The Ottawa River must be the short cut.

"I swear it is so!" Vignau had said.

And so Vignau was with Champlain and three other Frenchmen as they started up the Ottawa. A sixth man with them was an Indian who could speak French as well as the Indian tongues.

As they passed the place where Ottawa, the capital of Canada, now stands, Champlain thought it would be a fine place for a settlement. The river beyond there became very rough, with many rocks. The river churned about, and the current was swift.

Often the men walked on the shore and pulled the two canoes with ropes made of strips of elkskin. Champlain almost lost his life one day when the current suddenly pulled the canoe about. Champlain, with the rope wound around his hand, fell into the river and was dragged onto the rocks.

As the six men drew near to Lake Alumette, where an Indian village was located, Champlain noticed that Vignau was behaving strangely. He stayed by himself a great deal. At other times, he tried to get Champlain to go into dangerous places, saying that they were not as bad as they looked.

Once, when Champlain was alone in a canoe, he

asked Vignau about the rapids and falls that were ahead.

"They drop only a few feet, and then the water is peaceful. You can make it easily," Vignau said.

When Champlain drew near enough to see for himself, he barely had time to get to shore. Had he gone over the falls, he would have been dashed against rocks and killed.

"I forgot they were that bad," Vignau lied.

At Lake Alumette, the Indians were amazed at the sight of the men who had come up the river so far. When Champlain told them where they were going, and the story that Vignau had told him, the Indian chief shook his head. The Indians talked fast among themselves.

Champlain's Indian listened. His face grew troubled as he turned to his leader.

"Master," he said, "these Indians say that there is no sea at the end of this river. They say that no man should go farther, for there is only the wild river and Indians who kill. If you go farther north, the wild tribes will kill you with their charms and poisons, if not with their arrows!"

"They are lying," Champlain said. "Vignau was there. He saw with his own eyes." But even as he said this, Champlain thought of the many lies Vignau had told him. Could this be one more great lie?

"It is Vignau who lies," the Indian chief told him.

Champlain did not know whom to believe. Had he come all this way for nothing? Was Vignau making a fool of him?

"We will go on," he said. He got everything ready, watching Vignau as the men worked. When they were ready to start, he called Vignau to him.

"Vignau," he said, "I plan to go on to the place of which you told me. But, if I find that you have been lying to me, I will hang you from the nearest tree!"

Vignau saw the fierce look on Champlain's face. He could almost see his own dead body reflected in his leader's eyes.

"No, no!" he cried. "It is all a lie! I have never been up the river. I only heard about it from another—"

"Another liar!" shouted Champlain. "Get out of my sight! I never want to see you again!"

When his anger had quieted, Champlain listened to the words of the Indian chief.

"Go westward on the little river that flows into this wild one. At its end, a few miles of portage will take you to a lake and another river. That river empties into a sea so wide that you cannot see the other side."

Champlain thanked the chief and told him he would return to try that trail. He set up a cross and claimed the land for France before he left. Then back he went to the St. Lawrence River and down to Quebec.

It was two years before he could get back to Lake Alumette. Then he followed the chief's directions. He found himself on the shores of Georgian Bay, a great arm of Lake Huron. From there he went south and discovered the second of the Great Lakes to be explored, Lake Ontario.

Champlain explored many streams and parts of the land around the Great Lakes, making maps as he did so. His work set a pattern for other French explorers. All of the Great Lakes were found by them. They built trading posts as far west as Lake Superior. Priests came to New France, too, and opened missions.

The men who lived at the trading posts or went out hunting from them traveled far and wide. They were called *voyageurs,* or *coureurs du bois,* (runners of the woods) because they traveled so much. They learned to live as the Indians did, and often married Indian girls. Their sons hunted and trapped as their fathers had done, and spoke half Indian, half French.

The voyageurs explored the land far and wide, for many miles around the Great Lakes. Added to their work in mapping America were the travels of other great French explorers.

Nicollet explored and built posts around Lake Superior and Lake Michigan. Father Marquette, one of the priests, and a young man named Jolliet traveled south from Lake Michigan, through the Fox River, and into the Wisconsin River to the Mississippi. They went south as far as the part of the river where De Soto had been. Robert La Salle found the Ohio River and later went all the way down the Mississippi to its mouth.

French names over thousands of miles of North American land show the part the explorers of France played in mapping America. Their search for the Northwest Passage never opened the route to China, but it opened the great waterways of a new land.

Explorations

CARTIER
CHAMPLAIN . . . LASALLE
MARQUETTE and JOLIET

THE HALF MOON
ON THE
HUDSON

While Champlain was exploring the Great Lakes, there was an Englishman who came to leave his name on maps of North America.

"Why has the course been changed, Mister?" Captain Henry Hudson asked. His ship, the *Half Moon,* was heading back the way it had come, southward to the coast of Norway.

The man at the wheel shook his head. Without looking at Hudson, he said, "The men won't go on, Captain. They say nothing but ice lies ahead. We'll sit on a frozen sea until we are all as stiff as the frozen sails."

Captain Henry Hudson turned on his heel and went to his cabin. He knew he should give firm orders for the ship to follow the course the Dutch company who owned it had ordered. He was supposed to be finding a way through the north seas to China, by going over the North Pole.

Hudson had sailed northward twice before, trying to find a Northwest Passage for his own country, England, which had not wanted to let France and Spain get all the glory of discovery. He had asked the Dutch company if he could try a different course because of the ice and cold.

"Now, Captain Hudson," it was explained to him, "all you have to do is make your way through a few miles of ice. Then you will have clear sailing in open water over the North Pole."

Hudson shook his head. "Sir, the ice gets thicker as you go farther north. It can squeeze a ship until the timbers break into pieces no larger than matchsticks!"

The Company man grew impatient. "Follow our orders, Captain Hudson. Over the pole is the shortest way, as anyone can tell by looking at a globe. As to the ice, when you reach that part of the earth where the sun shines five months of the year, with no darkness at all, there cannot be much ice. The sunshine going on so long is bound to have melted it."

And so, in the same year that Samuel Champlain was going with the Indians to meet the Iroquois near Lake Champlain, Henry Hudson found himself sailing a route that he knew was wrong. He couldn't blame his men for their mutiny.

The next day, he met with his half-English, half-Dutch crew. His first mate, John Colman, was the only man who had sailed with him before. Mr. Colman stood at his side.

"We shall be laughed at if we return to Holland now," said Captain Hudson. "We have been sailing for two months, and we have gone nowhere. I agree that to go north is foolish. I shall give you your choice of two courses. We shall go west to the American coast, in any case."

Mr. Colman held a map to which the captain pointed.

"We can go around the north end of North America. Or we can go to try to find a passage through North America. Captain John Smith, of my country, has begun a colony. He reports many large river mouths along the coast. One of them must surely go through the continent."

It took the sailors no time at all to decide. They chose the southern course to get away from cold weather.

"Set the course, Mr. Colman," Captain Hudson ordered. And so it was because of a mutiny that Henry

Hudson found the river that has his name.

Other men had passed Long Island and the mouth of the Hudson River, but none had entered it. Hudson's *Half Moon* reached the coast of Newfoundland and then sailed south as far as John Smith's colony at Chesapeake Bay. They turned back north, and on the return trip dropped anchor somewhere south of Long Island on the night of September 2, 1609.

The next morning, John Colman stood at the rail, trying to see what was ahead. Captain Hudson joined him.

"The mists hang on this morning, Captain," said Colman. "They are just beginning to lift."

"Proceed northward, but slowly," the Captain ordered.

"Anchors aweigh!" called the mate. He moved to the wheel to set the course as two sailors began to turn the spool-like capstan on the deck to wind up the anchor line.

Men climbed up the masts, and soon a few of the *Half Moon's* sails were opened to the breeze that was lifting the mists from the water. Captain Hudson liked what he could see, a wide harbor between the cliffs of

Long Island and the flatter coast of what was to be New Jersey. The next morning they were tied near the island's end. Indians on the shore were singing songs of welcome.

A canoe-load of Indians came to the ship with gifts of plums, corn, and huckleberries. Hudson let them come on board the ship to see what it was like. Before they had left, he gave them some of the knives and beads he had brought with him as trading goods.

Some of the crew of the *Half Moon* made fun of the Indians and their strange ways. They were the same sailors who had gone ashore in New England and stolen from the Indians' houses. They had even stolen a boat the French had given the Indians.

Word of the unfriendly ways of some of the crew of the *Half Moon* spread quickly. The next day, as they reached the place where the bay comes in to form "The Narrows," the first real trouble came.

Captain Hudson called John Colman to him in the morning.

"Take the small boat and go ahead to see if the waters widen again and if the ship can get through," he said.

Coleman and four sailors set off to the north in the rowboat. They had been gone almost all day when they saw that the waters did widen again, to form what is now New York harbor. Before they started back, they decided to rest awhile. The air was sweet with autumn wild flowers. Butterflies danced about, and all seemed peaceful.

Just then, there was a whizzing sound. John Coleman yelled as a stone arrow hit his throat. Then he fell forward, dying. As more arrows fell, the sailors saw two canoes of Indians hurrying shoreward.

Night closed in on the men. The tide, coming in from the sea, pushed against their boat. They moved along as best they could in the darkness. It was ten o'clock in the morning when they reached the *Half Moon* and lifted the dead mate up to the deck. He was buried later in the day not far from Sandy Hook.

"We'll be on guard from now on," Hudson said. He missed his only friend on the ship, John Colman. In his place as mate was a Dutch sailor.

Just before they lifted anchor to head northward, the men on the *Half Moon* had more Indian visitors. They locked up two of them when the rest were leaving the ship. As the ship went through New York harbor, the sailors put red coats on the Indians and made them dance.

"Haw, haw!" laughed the sailors. "Don't that beat all."

Each day, the Indian's faces showed more and more hatred for the sailors. At the end of a week, they escaped through a porthole and swam to shore.

In the meantime, the *Half Moon* had gone past the places where great cities were to rise and past the place where West Point would some day be. The sailors saw the Catskill Mountains.

Above the place where Albany was to rise, the river turned. Hudson sent the small boat ahead to get a report.

"It will not lead us to the sea, Captain," the mate reported. "It grows smaller rather than larger. We would do well to turn back."

Henry Hudson sighed. For the third time, he had been unable to find the Northwest Passage. "Turn back," he said.

On October 2, the *Half Moon* was back at anchor near the mouth of the Hudson River. As soon as the ship stopped, several canoe-loads of Indians had put out from shore. The man who kept the records, Mr. Juet, stood beside the captain.

"Look," he said, "that Indian is one of the two we kidnapped. Trouble may be ahead."

The first canoe pulled alongside the ship, and the Indians signalled that they would like to come on board.

Hudson said, "No. Speak from where you are."

All the canoes had stopped. As soon as the watching Indians saw Hudson shake his head, bows were lifted, and a shower of arrows rattled onto the deck.

"Drop down!" someone called. The men flattened themselves on the deck, or hid behind coils of rope and chests.

Then the captain called out, "Get your guns and fire!"

The men had to aim at the Indians' backs, for they had turned about and were hurrying to the shore. About one hundred more had suddenly appeared on a high point of land overlooking the harbor.

"The falcon!" Juet cried. "The falcon will reach them!"

The "falcon" was the largest cannon on the ship. It had a mouth five inches across, and shot a ball weighing two and a half pounds. Just as a fresh shower of arrows hit the ship, there was a great roar. The sailors saw two Indians fall as the ball hit. The rest ran into the woods.

"There they go!" cried the mate, but Captain Hudson pointed to a large canoe in which nine men were paddling toward the ship as fast as they could.

"Juet! Turn the falcon downward!" he called and pointed to the canoe.

Juet aimed. In a moment, the canoe folded in the middle. Men flew from it. Only four reached the bank.

"Anchors aweigh!" the captain called. The sailors hurried to their positions at anchor and sail lines. The *Half Moon* moved out of the Hudson River forever.

Henry Hudson felt only discouragement. He had no idea of how important the shores he was leaving would become. Because of his journey, Holland had a claim in the New World and began what was to become its greatest city.

England took Hudson back into her service the next year, and sent him to America in another small ship, the *Discovery*. She headed westward, but farther north than the *Half Moon* had gone.

The *Discovery* swung into Hudson Strait. The farther north the ship went, the more frightened the sailors became. The sails froze into stiff sheets. Moving ice masses struck against the wooden ship. Again Hudson had mutiny on his hands. Just as the men became hard to handle, the ship swung southward into the great arm of the sea now known as Hudson's Bay.

But a turn in the weather brought more ice, even though they were going south. November came, and the men were frozen into James Bay. Food ran short. Many men became ill, and all were bored. They had nothing to do but think.

"He's holding back food that belongs to us," the men began to mutter. They looked angrily at Henry Hudson's closed cabin door. Almost all of the men turned against their leader.

In June, when the ice had freed the ship, they put the small boat into the water. They forced Henry Hudson and eight other men, mostly sick, to get into it. Then the thirteen men left on board the *Discovery*

raised the anchor and sailed away, leaving the nine men without food or water.

That is the last anyone ever heard of Henry Hudson, the man who had the courage of a discoverer, but did not know how to put fighting spirit into his men.

UP THE WIDE MISSOURI

When the new country, the United States of America, was begun, men had mapped the shape of North America. They had been all around the edges, except in the frozen Arctic region of the north. They knew how large the continent was, but there were great parts of the West where no white man had traveled.

The baby country was still struggling to stand on its own legs when suddenly it grew to almost twice its size. The first boundaries of the United States were the Atlantic Ocean on the east, the Mississippi River on the west, the Great Lakes on the north, and the Gulf of Mexico to the south. But in 1803, the United States bought a great piece of land in the west. It included the rest of the Mississippi River valley and the valley of the Missouri River.

The people, and especially President Thomas Jefferson, wondered what the land was like. No one had an exact map of it. No one knew exactly how long the Missouri River was or where it started.

"Does it connect with the Columbia River?" people wondered. "Can you go from the Missouri right into the Columbia and down to the Pacific Ocean?"

President Jefferson decided to send explorers up the Missouri River. In May, 1804, Captain Meriwether Lewis and Captain William Clark, with forty-four men, left St. Louis, Missouri. They had a keelboat and two small boats, loaded with food, tools, ammunition, clothing and plenty of gifts for the Indians.

The boatmen pulled the boats up the Missouri River, usually walking on the shore dragging the boats with ropes, for the current was very strong. When winter came and the river began to have ice in it, they had reached the place where Bismarck, North Dakota, is today. In those days, it was open plain, except for groves of cottonwood trees near the river. The villages of the Mandan Indians were near by.

"We'll make our winter camp here," the two captains decided.

When spring came, they watched for the breaking of the ice. On Friday, March 29, 1805, the river roared with rushing chunks of ice. The men began to get ready to move on. They loaded the keelboat with things to send back to St. Louis, for they would not

take it farther up the river. They sent stuffed animals and animal skeletons and skins to the President of the United States, along with maps and reports on what they had seen so far.

More than two months and almost nine hundred miles up the Missouri River from their winter camp, they came to a place where the river forked.

"Which way, Captain?" asked Peter Cruzatte, one of the boatmen.

Captain Lewis looked at the two streams of water. The water of the north river was the color of the Missouri as they had come to know it, muddy and gray. On the other hand, the south river was wider and deeper, although its waters were clear.

"What do you think, Captain Clark?" he asked.

Big William Clark took off his cap and scratched his head until his red hair stood on end. He looked at one and then at the other. Much depended upon their making the right choice, for the Indians had told them that the Missouri River began not far from the Columbia's beginning on the other side of the Rocky Mountain slope. They planned to go down the Columbia to the Pacific Ocean.

While Clark was thinking it over, Cruzatte spoke up. "I think the north river is the Missouri," he said.

Captain Clark had made up his mind, too. "I think it is the south river."

"Well," said Captain Lewis, "we shall have to send parties up each river to make sure. The Indians told us there were great waterfalls in the true Missouri River, and they should not be many miles from here."

The next morning, Tuesday, June 4, each of the two captains set out with a few men to explore the rivers. Captain Lewis was to follow the north river, and Captain Clark the south. A few men, those whose feet were most blistered, stayed in camp. They would repair the ropes for the canoes, for several times lately the ropes had broken as the canoes were being dragged up the river.

When Captain Lewis, with his six men, had been walking up the banks of the north river for two days, he felt sure that it was not the true Missouri. It swung too far to the north. That day, Thursday, the rain began about noon, coming unpleasantly on gusts of wind. The men had just begun their return trip. The banks were becoming slippery, so they threw some rafts together to float down the river.

They started out, three men and their packs to a raft. But the water washed onto the rafts too badly, and the current swung them about. They gave up the rafts and went ashore. They began the long walk.

"Be careful on this one!" Captain Lewis called. He was leading the men. They had come to a place where they had to walk on a slippery, wet shelf of rock, about ninety feet above the river. The cliff dropped almost straight down below them.

Captain Lewis started on the thirty-foot-long ledge. He was past the narrowest part and beginning to breathe more easily when he heard one of his men calling.

"Captain! What shall I do?"

Captain Lewis placed his back against the rock wall and turned his head. There, about halfway across the ledge, was Dick Windsor, lying face down. His right arm and leg hung over the edge of the shelf above the river, while he held on with his left hand and foot.

The captain kept himself from crying out in fear.

"You are in no danger, Dick," he said when he

could keep his voice steady. "Just pull your knife from your belt with your right hand."

He watched as Dick did as he was told. "Now reach down as far as your arm hangs and cut a toe hold for yourself in the ledge," the captain said.

Carefully, Dick worked at the rock and soil. The other five men waited and watched at the other end of the pass. Dick eased his right foot toward the hole he had cut. No one spoke. Carefully, Dick pulled himself into a kneeling position on the ledge.

"That's the way, Dick," Captain Lewis said. "Now take off your moccasins and come forward on your hands and knees."

Dick stuffed his moccasins, slippery with mud, into his belt, keeping his eye on the ledge just ahead. With his knife in one hand and his rifle in the other, he crawled toward Captain Lewis. When the two of them reached a wider path, the waiting men cheered.

"Go back and down to the river," Captain Lewis called to them. "Wade in the river past this place."

From then on, the men stayed off high, narrow ledges.

The rain went on, all through the day and into the

night. The men had killed a deer, which they cooked when they made camp. The night before, they had slept outdoors in the rain. This night they found an old Indian lodge and slept inside on some willow boughs. At five o'clock Saturday evening they reached the camp where the other men waited.

"I am sure the north river is not the Missouri," Captain Lewis said as he marked it on the map. "I believe I'll name it Maria's River."

Captain Clark had returned earlier from his trip up the south river fork. "I agree with you," he said. "I think the south river is the true Missouri."

He and his men had gone far enough to see that the river went on just as wide as before and in the right direction. Cruzatte and some of the other men still thought the north river was the Missouri.

"We will go where you say, Captains, but we think the south river will end this side of the first mountains," said Cruzatte.

Captain Lewis said, "We must find out if there are falls in the south river. If there are, we can be sure it is the Missouri. I shall go ahead on foot far enough to find the falls or the mountains."

Before he left he suggested they dig holes in high ground and hide part of the supplies. It would lighten their loads and they would need the supplies on the return trip. The faster water of the river would make it harder to pull the canoes from the fork onward.

Capain Lewis took four men and went on ahead. The others were to start with the boats when they were ready. On the third day out, Captain Lewis and his men heard a roaring sound. Seven miles farther, they saw the falls of the Missouri River.

At first the men could say nothing at the beautiful sight.

"How high would you guess they are?" one of the men asked.

Captain Lewis said, "There must be an eighty-foot fall of water there."

In order to plan how they would pass the falls with their canoes, they went on farther. They soon found that there was not just one waterfall, but a series of them.

That same day, Captain Lewis was away from the other men when he saw a herd of buffalo. He shot one for meat. He stood a moment and watched it fall as the rest of the herd went on. A noise behind him caused him to turn. There was a huge bear coming toward him.

"I didn't reload my gun!" Captain Lewis remembered.

He looked about for a place to hide. There wasn't a tree to climb or a rock large enough to hide behind. There was only the river. In that moment, the bear caught his scent. He growled and began running toward the captain.

Captain Lewis waited no longer. He ran towards the river. Twenty feet out and waist deep he stopped and turned to see where the bear was. He lifted his gun to load it, and as he did so, the bear turned and ran.

"I must look very fierce," he thought. "But I've learned a lesson. Never leave a rifle unloaded for even a few minutes when you're in country like this!"

Before he got back to camp, three buffalo bulls, feeding with a herd a half mile away, caught his scent. To Captain Lewis' surprise, they began charging fiercely toward him.

"I can't run from them, and I can't load my gun fast enough to shoot all three," the captain thought.

"I'll have to try what I did with the bear."

He faced the buffaloes and, holding his knife before him, began walking toward them. The three beasts stopped suddenly, about a hundred yards from the captain. They looked at him a few minutes, and then they turned and headed back to the herd.

"What a day this has been," Captain Lewis thought. He headed back to camp, not knowing what adventure would come next.

And so the trip went on. The hard-working men dragged the boats to the waterfalls. There they pulled them ashore. They cut down a big cottonwood tree and sawed it into slices to make wheels. They made rough carts on which to load the dugout canoes to carry them up the hills until they were past the waterfalls.

When the falls had been passed, there were the Rocky Mountains to climb. Later they had to leave their canoes altogether. There were Indian tribes to satisfy, and the Columbia River to find and travel to the Pacific Ocean.

By the time they had done this and then returned to St. Louis, they had traveled 8,000 miles. The great unknown West was no longer unknown. What they

told of it drew hundreds of adventurers in the next few years.

SEA
OF
SALT

Lewis and Clark were on their way back down the Missouri River when their stories of wonderful hunting and trapping lands reached the ears of men with adventure in their souls. More stories came back with the men who had been sent west with Zebulon Pike to where Colorado is now. Pike had been sent by the government to explore south of the Missouri River.

It did not matter to the hundreds of trappers who headed west that there were great blank spaces on the maps. Unknown ground did not frighten them. They followed the rivers. Where the rivers went, they went. When the river they were following no longer held enough beavers, they moved on until they found another river with plenty of "beaver signs." In that way, the trappers helped fill in the blank spaces on the map with what they learned about the west.

A group of men who trapped for the Rocky Mountain Fur Company were camping in the valley of the Bear River in the winter of 1824 to 1825. They had trapped their way down Bear River from its beginning in southern Idaho. They were almost to where the Idaho-Utah boundary is now when they got to talking about Bear River one night as they sat around their campfire.

"Where does Bear River go?" young Jim Bridger asked. He was a newcomer to the trapper's company.

"Can't tell you, Jim," said Mr. Ashley, one of the company owners. "No one has followed it any farther than this."

"It could be the River Buenaventure," one of the men said. "Buenaventure" was a river of which everyone had heard, but which no one had seen. It was on the old Spanish maps as a river which led through the Rocky Mountains to the Pacific Ocean. The old dream of an easy passage to the western sea was still alive.

"More likely it is a river which joins those which run into the Missouri River," said another trapper.

The men had little to do, and they spent a long time arguing about where the Bear River went.

"Let's settle it," said Mr. Ashley. "We'll send a man down the river to find out."

He looked around at the faces of the men, lighted

by the campfire. One looked eager. It was the face of young Jim Bridger.

"Jim, how would you like to settle this question for us? Take the dugout canoe and go exploring for a day or two," Mr. Ashley said.

Jim looked pleased to be chosen. "Take care of my traps for me, and I'll be glad to go," he said.

The next morning, Jim took a leather pouch of "jerked" buffalo meat and his blanket, rifle, knife and ax. He set off down the river to be an explorer.

His paddle dipped slowly and regularly into the cold water of the river. Even the river seemed hushed as he moved out of earshot of his camp-mates. The silence deepened. Jim had never felt so alone. He was glad when a muskrat slipped into the water with a little splash. It was good to know there was another living creature near.

The river narrowed and deepened as canyon walls closed it in. The current became swifter, and Jim had to work hard with the paddle to keep the canoe from hitting the rocks which now and then stuck up above the water. Swirling waters pulled at the canoe and tried to swing it about.

"I think I had better find out what is ahead," Jim said aloud. He watched for a place where he could get to shore and climb the bank. The rock wall sloped off, and Jim saw his chance.

He tied the canoe to a young tree at the water's edge and climbed the bank. Then he went up the side of a hill on which a tall pine grew. He climbed the tree as high as he could.

His eyes followed the river. Just beyond this rough place it widened. The steep canyon walls gentled into rolling hills. And there, spreading out from the river's mouth was water reaching as far as his eyes could see.

"A sea!" Jim cried. As he came quickly down the tree the thought went through his head, "Perhaps this *is* the Buenaventure, and beyond is the Pacific Ocean. I shall be the one who discovered it!"

His heart beat fast as he untied his canoe and pushed off. He paddled fast, eager to reach the sea.

The sun was low as he came to the river's end. Jim beached the canoe, noticing as he did so the strange white coating of the sand. He knelt down at the water's edge and scooped up a handful to taste.

"Ugh!" he spat it out quickly and hurried back to

a spring he had noticed trickling into the river. Then, as he rinsed his mouth and drank of the fresh water, it came to him.

"This is a salt sea! I have found the Pacific Ocean."

The idea made it hard for him to go to sleep after he had eaten the dried meat and rolled up in his blanket. He was awake before the sun was up. He took one last look at the wide stretch of water and turned towards camp. He could reach it faster going overland than paddling against the river's current.

But the men laughed when he rushed in with his excited cry, "I've found the Pacific Ocean! Bear River is Buenaventure!"

Then, because he seemed too earnest to be playing a joke, the men decided to check Jim's story. The next day, several of them went down to the salt sea. There was no doubt, Jim had found a body of salt water.

But one of the men had seen the Pacific Ocean. "No, Jim," he said, "you haven't found a new way to the Pacific Ocean. The ocean has a wilder look to it. This must be an inland salt sea."

The next year, a few men paddled all around the shore of the sea. They found that Jim's "ocean" was an

inland lake, some strange leftover of the days when North America was mostly covered by an ocean. It was named the Great Salt Lake. There was no river connecting the lake with the ocean.

Ashley's next reports to the government showed the location of the lake, and it became an important place in later years. Jim Bridger went on exploring more of the face of the West, as the other trappers did. His fort which he built in later years became one of the landmarks which helped guide the wagon trains.

SEARCH
FOR THE
BUENAVENTURE

Among the trappers, young but seeming old, was a man named Jedediah Smith. Jed was always looking for more than the money and adventure that beaver trapping brought him. He wanted to make his life worth living through doing something to help his fellow man.

Jed and his men sat near their campfire on the last night of the great *rendezvous* of 1826, not far from Jim Bridger's newly discovered Great Salt Lake. The trappers from far and wide came together once a year at some mountain valley. There the fur-trading company men came with packs of supplies and money to trade for the furs. The yearly get-together was called the *rendezvous,* the French word for *meeting*.

Another trapper, Bob Evans, sat beside Jed. A group of men at a near-by campfire had just finished singing a rowdy mountain song. In the sudden quiet, Bob's thoughts went to the trip the men were to begin at dawn.

"Jed," he asked, "what are the plans for our trip?"

Jed Smith closed the worn, leather-covered Bible which was always as near him as his rifle. He rubbed his eyes, tired from reading in the flickering fire-light.

"Well, Bob," he said, "I plan to cut south and a little west. I would like to find the headwaters of the River Buenaventure. Just think what that would mean to men in all the years to come! If there is a river to the Pacific, as every old Spanish map shows, then there must also be a pass through the Rocky Mountains. The river would have cut a canyon through which to flow."

Bob pictured the great Buenaventure filled with boats carrying people swiftly across the miles. "We should be able to find it, Jed," he said. The loud singing began again. Near another campfire, a circle was forming around two men who were about to have a rough-and-tumble fist fight.

"We're on our way before sun-up," Jed told his men. He stood up and stretched his tall, lean body. The fire-light threw his shadow far towards the next campfire and lost it there. Smith took his blanket and spread it on the ground. Soon he and his sixteen men were rolled up like a collection of cocoons spread out on the ground. The noise of the big camp seemed not to bother them at all.

Early in the morning, there was no trace of them except flattened grass and the ashes where the fire had been. The seventeen men were miles away, a long string with the fifty horses and mules that carried their packs. Mile after mile they headed southward. By noon each day, men and animals were so hot and thirsty that they moved in silence. No sounds broke the silence but the squeak of saddle leather and the clop of hoofs.

Now and then, Jed Smith would ride away from the group to a high point from which he could see for miles. There he would stop his horse. His blue eyes would narrow that he might see the countryside for miles around, ever seeking the River Buenaventure.

In the evening, when the horses had been watered and fed and buffalo meat roasted over the fire for the men to eat, Jed would go off by himself again, his Bible in his hand. The light in his eye when he came back told the rough trappers that Jed's praying had brought him courage, even though he had found no stream that could be the Buenaventure. Somehow, the courage was passed along to the other sixteen men.

The men's beards were long and their hair rough and matted when at last they reached the Colorado River. They were deep into Spanish territory by that time. Smith had long given up looking for the Buenaventure, because the maps showed it lying farther north.

Westward, then, they went, until at last they reached the Pacific coast in southern California. There the Spanish priests had built missions long ago and, in the valleys, Spanish ranchers raised beef cattle. The winter months had come. The men had been traveling since early summer. They set up camp there in California.

Late in May of 1827, Jed Smith chose two men to go back with him to Utah, seeking the Buenaventure on the way. One was Silas Gobel, big and strong from many years of working as a blacksmith. Bob Evans, Jed's closest friend, was the other. The rest of the men would stay to trap in the streams of northern California.

Jed, Bob and Si would head almost due east, this time, except for the many turns and twists that would be necessary in order to pick a way through the Sierra

Nevada mountain range. They started out with seven horses and a pair of mules.

"Look at the mules trying to reach the hay on their own backs!" Si laughed. The two mules carried a supply of hay for the horses on those days when there would be no grass near the night's camping place. They looked foolish now as they stretched their necks and bit at their own loads at the same time that they moved forward.

Hearing the men laugh, they kicked their heels and brayed, trying harder than ever to loosen their loads so that they could have a feast. Bob Evans, bringing up the end of the long line, urged them along. Si rode alongside the middle of the pack string, and Jed led the way on his little brown mare on which he had traveled many, many miles.

The California valleys gave plenty of food for the animals when the days were over. Men and animals both rested well under the starry sky. But each day, the going was harder as they entered the mountain range. Higher and higher they went, dropping now and then into valleys between the peaks, but often seeing the snow which stayed all year on the higher mountains.

One day they were threading their way along a rocky shelf of a canyon wall. There was no tried and true trail for them to follow, for no white man had gone this way before them. As they started through a canyon, they could not be sure that there would be a passable way out of it.

The rocky, snow-covered ledge turned and seemed to be narrowing into nothing. Under the covering of snow, there were loose stones on the steep slope. The snow lay drifted and heavy in the valley below.

"No way to go but down!" Jed called back. "Here goes!"

But his little mare was not ready. She felt her front feet sliding at the first step. She pulled back, pawing and shaking her head.

"Come on, girl," Smith said. "Take it easy and you can make it." He patted her neck.

She started down then, her knees stiff as she felt the stones and snow sliding under her. Trying to walk, but mostly sliding on her tail, she led the way for the other horses. One by one, they started down as the slack in the rope was taken up.

At the end of the line, Bob Evans was having trouble with the mules. As the slack in the rope tightened, they dug their hoofs into the ground and bellowed, holding back the whole pack.

"Get along there!" Bob called to them, and tugged at the bridle of the leading mule.

Bob pushed and the weight of the horses below pulled. Suddenly, whether they willed it or not, the mules moved forward and down, faster than any of the horses had gone.

"Whoa!" yelled Bob, for the mules were tumbling headlong against the horses strung along the slope.

The whole string went into a fast tumble. Snow flew until it looked like a blizzard going on below. Packs, saddles, horses legs and flying tails poked out like quills on a rolling porcupine.

Bob Evans, watching from above, saw the snow gradually settle.

"Jed! Si!" he called. "Are you all right?"

And then he could see for himself. Big Si was rolling about, free of the kicking horses. Jed was picking himself up, brushing the cold snow from inside his collar. Bob set his horse to sliding down the slope to join the others.

The three men looked at one another, and at the mess of packs, saddles and tangled lines. Then they burst out laughing.

"What a ridiculous mess!" said Jed. "This is one trail we won't try again."

"Baw-w-w-w-w-w!" trumpeted a mule, and the men laughed again. They set to work.

Some time later, the horses stood ready with packs in place. "Let us thank God no one was hurt," said Jed, "and then be on our way."

That day and for many days to follow, the three men picked their way over the mountains and through the valleys. High winds pushed stinging snow into their faces. There was little to shelter them or their animals against the cold of night. By the time they made their way to the desert beyond the mountains, men and animals alike were worn and thin.

The cold of the mountains was strange to remember as the hot sun beat down on them day after day. Their water gave out, and there was no sign of a river ahead.

"The Buenaventure should be near," Jed told them. "If we do not find it soon, it does not exist." As before, he looked often, far and wide, for a sight of the river.

Bob felt his head swimming under the open sky and the hot sun. He stopped his horse to rest a moment and then looked up. "Mountains! Mountains and a cool lake ahead!" he called.

Jed looked ahead where Bob pointed, peering into the desert emptiness.

He shook his head. "No, Bob. A *mirage* is all you see. When we get there, you will find there is no mountain and no lake."

They went on, plodding slowly along. The first of their horses who were to die dropped along the way.

And then, at last, real mountains were ahead, with a thunderstorm promising blessed rain. Men, horses and mules took new spirit.

In a few days, there was desert again. The supply of water was almost gone, and none was in sight. No one knew how far ahead water lay. The men's tongues grew thick, and they could not eat the strips of dry meat which were all they had. Each day they grew thinner, and their eyes sank back into their heads.

Day after day, they went on. Even Jed gave up hoping to find the Buenaventure. But he did not give up going off by himself each day to read his Bible and pray.

One day, Bob Evans dropped to the ground. His horse had died days before, and the one horse and one mule that were still alive were too weak to carry a man.

"Bob, just a little way more. Come on, Bob!" Jed said. He and Si tried to lift the fallen man, but they could not do it.

Jed's eyes were the eyes of a man of ninety as he said, "We'll have to leave him, Si." He dropped to his knees. "Yea, though I walk through the valley of death—"

After a few minutes, he rose and stumbled on, not looking back at Bob Evans, his dearest friend. And then, within the hour, as if in answer to Jed's prayer, they found a fresh spring of water. Silas stayed with the horse and the mule, and Jed, carrying a kettle of water, went back to Bob.

The three men reached Great Salt Lake not long after, and headed northward to Bear Lake and the rendezvous camp. There they rested until they were strong enough for the new adventures which lay ahead.

Jed and his men traveled the length of the Pacific coast from southern California to the Columbia River. They followed that river and a section of the Rocky Mountains where no white man had gone before them. Jed kept records which he sent to the government so that all men who came later should profit from his explorations.

In 1831, thirty-three year old Jed started on what he said would be his last trip. He had said that in 1830, too, but in St. Louis he had found his brothers wanting to go on a trapping venture in order to get the money they needed. Jed turned his back on the rest he had planned to take and headed west once more. But one day, as he was bent over to dig under the sand for water, some Comanche Indians shot him in the back.

Jed's life was gone, but not until his courage had brought new light to the great unknown West.

MAPPING THE WESTWARD TRAILS

The old mountain men who lived on after Jed Smith was gone combed the smallest streams in the farthest valleys for beaver signs. But each year there were fewer of the little animals, and around 1840 most of the beavers had disappeared from the Far West.

By that time, the first cries of "Westward to Oregon!" were heard. A few brave people made the long, long journey across the plains and the mountains. They used the mountain men's trails, and asked them the way to go.

There were maps, but none of them drew together all that the trappers had learned. The United States Government gave the work of mapping the westward trails to a young man named John Charles Fremont.

It was a bit of luck that brought Kit Carson, trapper and western traveler, onto the steamboat on which Lt. Fremont was riding just as he was about to start his first trip west. Fremont needed a guide. Kit Carson needed work. That was in 1842, and it was the beginning of a long friendship.

"Do you know the West?" Fremont had asked the mountain man.

Kit, brown and toughened by years of living in the open, straightened his broad shoulders. If there were any man alive who knew the West, Kit Carson was that man!

"Lt. Fremont," he said, "I've trapped the streams from the northern Rockies to the southern deserts. I've journeyed many times to the Spanish country around Santa Fe. From there I've gone westward to the Colorado River and on to California, and northward to the Columbia River. I know the streams of the Wind River Mountain country, where you are going, as well as I know the veins on my own hand."

He held out that leathery hand and Fremont took it in his smoother city man's hand. They sealed a bargain and their first of several trips together began.

Kit Carson became John Fremont's "right hand man." When Fremont was unsure which way to go, Kit told him what lay ahead. When the alarm came that Indians were near. Kit was ready on his horse, rifle in hand, to scout, fight or settle matters peacefully. His knowledge of the West, gathered in seventeen years as a trapper, made Kit Carson a good man to have around.

The first trip took them to the Wind River Mountains in what is now western Wyoming. Fremont and Carson led a line of about twenty-five men. One man was an expert map-maker. The others were "voyageurs" or mountain men like Kit, hired to hunt meat animals for the men.

Each day, Fremont made notes of the path they followed, the plants and animals they saw and what the land was like. He measured the temperature, how high the land rose and where the day's march had brought them. The map-maker made his records, too. When the first journey was over, a great part of the Oregon Trail had been mapped, including a pass through the first range of mountains.

When he heard that Fremont, now a captain, was beginning a second journey into the West, Carson hurried to join him. This time they were going farther west. First they went to Great Salt Lake. There Carson helped Fremont explore Fremont Island in the lake. They almost lost their lives trying to get back to the mainland in stormy weather, for their boat leaked as fast as the men could bail it out.

From Great Salt Lake, they followed more of the Oregon Trail to the Columbia River. Another old mountaineer, Thomas Fitzpatrick, joined them for this part of the trip. He and Kit Carson worked together to help the little band of men live through the hard days that were to come.

Winter was almost upon them when the men were ready to leave the Columbia River country and go back home. They did not go back the way they had come, for Fremont was still holding to an old dream. He, too, had seen the Spanish maps with the River Buenaventure cutting through the mountains to the Pacific Ocean.

"We'll head south to the Buenaventure, for we are sure to come to it on that route. That will be a big help to people traveling to the Pacific Ocean," Fremont told his men. He did not know that a fur-company man named Captain Bonneville had just traveled that country. Bonneville had decided, as Jed Smith had, that there was no such river.

As the men were getting ready to break camp, Kit Carson thought of the winters he had spent in the West.

"A winter in the mountains is worse than you would guess," he told Captain Fremont.

"But we won't have to spend a winter in the mountains, Carson," said Fremont. "When we find the Buenaventure, we will winter in its grassy valley where there is food for both men and horses. When the spring grasses grow, we will start eastward."

So the men, riding horses and mules and leading pack animals, started south and east in early December, 1843. Snow soon began to fall. Traveling through the mountains and the pine forests was slow.

On Christmas morning, they were camped on the shore of a mountain lake. The best way they could think of to mark the day was by shooting a salute from all their guns. Having done that, they went on their way as they did on other days.

A month later they had passed many more lakes and rivers. They had made their way to lower ground at the foot of the mountains. Each time he saw a stream, Captain Fremont's hopes rose that it would be the Buenaventure, for they had reached the part of the country where the Spanish maps showed the river to be.

"Ride ahead, Carson," he would say to Kit. "See if that is the Buenaventure." But each time, Carson returned shaking his head. "Beaver signs aren't right for a river going to the Pacific," he would say.

Late in January, Fremont discovered that his horses could not go much farther in rocky country. Their shoes were falling off, and there were no more nails to put them back on. The horses were lamer each day, and there was little food left for them on the days when grass could not be found.

He called the men together around the campfire that night. For the first time, Fremont's shoulders sagged and the light was gone from his black eyes.

"I have given up hope of finding the River Buenaventure," he said. "There is no use looking for it any farther south. We must get to good pasture and a place where we can find food for ourselves very soon. Instead of starting eastward across the desert and the plains and more mountains, I have decided that we should find a pass through these mountains to the west. The Sacramento River valley should be just over the mountains, and there we shall find the homes of white men."

A great cheer rose from the men. The next morning, they were all in good spirits as they started the search for the pass through the mountains. Neither Kit Carson nor Fitzpatrick knew this part of the Sierra Nevadas.

"Indians could tell us," Carson said. But when the men saw Indian huts, they were always empty. Inside the huts would be baskets, a rabbit skin or two, matted grasses, and a fire still sending lazy smoke through the hole in the middle of the roof. Sometimes they would see the last Indians running away to hide.

The explorers moved on. Smoke signals rising from the valleys told of Indians spreading the word of their coming. Then one morning an old Indian came running into the camp as the men were getting ready to leave. The Indian had decided to risk his life to learn what the white men were doing in his land.

The old Indian reached out and took the hand of the first man he came to as a sign of friendship. He held out a skin bag with a few pounds of small nuts in it. They were the kernels which the Indians shook out of a certain kind of pine tree.

Fremont tried one of the nuts.

"It is good," he said as he passed the bag to the other men. "Get some of that red cloth for this fellow."

The Indian looked pleased with the gift. Fremont started a long talk in sign language, trying to make the Indian understand that he wanted a guide to help find the way through the mountains. More Indians came into the camp. They understood what Fremont wanted, and when the men broke camp three of them went along. They stayed with the men long enough to start them into the mountains.

From then on, Indians came to the camp with the bags of nuts to trade. One or two of them would go with Fremont, but only for a day or two. They always seemed to fear the Indians of the next valley, and the deep snow ahead. But the men were deep into the mountains and going higher each day before they were left with no Indian guide at all. Carson and Fitzpatrick went on short scouting trips each day to keep the long line of horses from having to pick its way through more miles of snow than necessary.

Soon there was little grass to be found for the animals. In the valleys, the snow lay deep. The rocky mountain sides had little growing upon them that the horses would eat.

One day Kit motioned to Fremont to ride close. They had just entered a valley, and Kit pointed to moving figures on the rocky walls.

"Look, Captain," said Kit. "Those Indians must be of a new tribe. Can you see the snowshoes they are wearing?"

Fremont saw that the men seemed to glide about on the deep snow. They stayed about as far away from the white men as an arrow could be shot, not knowing of the power of the guns to reach them if the white men had so chosen. On the ledges they perched, laughing aloud and watching the explorers.

But again, their wish to know about the white man brought them closer. A few came to the camp. The men saw that their snowshoes were made of hoops of green wood, cross-laced with stringy tree bark. The explorers made some for themselves.

A day or two later, Indians came into the camp carrying rabbits, and the long nets they set into the ground to catch them. Fremont gave them more of the red and blue cloth they seemed to like so well. Then he tried again to learn more of the way through the mountains. He took a stick and scratched pictures in the snow. He drew a valley and a white man's cabin. "How far?" he asked.

One of the Indians seemed to understand. He held up one finger and then closed his eyes as if in sleep. Six times he did this.

"Six sleeps to the white man's houses," Fremont said. Then he saw that the Indian was making more signs. He pointed to the snow. With his hand he showed snow getting deeper and deeper, until it was as high as a man's head, and then even higher. Then he turned to the east, away from the deeper snow. He made Fremont understand that there was a river to follow to a lake where a man could camp until spring.

"We are strong. Our horses are strong. We will make a road through the snow," Fremont told the Indian. Then he made more signs to ask for an Indian guide. It took many gifts to get one to agree to go along.

The men remembered how their last guide had been so cold that he ran back to his fire after one day. They dressed this Indian in leggings, moccasins, a shirt, and a large green blanket. They gave him red and blue cloth, too, but he would not wrap that about himself. He carried it rolled tightly.

The snow grew deeper as the Indians had warned. A man and a horse at the head of the line broke the way for the others until they were too tired. Then they rested, letting the next one break the way and all others pass before they rejoined the line.

Each day the job grew harder. The men cut pieces of log to make mauls with which to hammer down the snow, for the horses sank too deep to move. The cold winds blew the snow into the men's faces. There were few places where anything could be found for the horses to eat, and each day they grew thinner and weaker. The men, too, were growing thin, for all they had to eat was soup made from dried peas and melted snow and a few of the nuts the Indians had brought them.

One morning, Fremont saw the Indian guide standing by the fire, shivering with cold.

"Here, man. Here's another blanket," Fremont said, and put his blanket around the Indian's shoulders. That was the last Fremont saw of him. When he looked for him a few minutes later to ask the way, the guide was gone.

Fremont, Carson and Fitzpatrick set out on another scouting trip to find the way. The rest of the men stayed in camp making more snowshoes and some sleds. The horses were too weak to carry the packs, and the men planned to pull their goods on the sleds.

The scouts had gone about ten miles ahead of the camp when they reached the top of a peak. Far below lay a broad valley. Beyond it, about one hundred miles away, rose another mountain range.

"That's it!" cried Carson. "Those are the last mountains before the green valley! Beyond them there is no snow!"

"How can you be sure?" Fremont asked.

Kit pointed to a certain peak. "See that little mountain? It is fifteen years since I last saw it, but I could never mistake it. I am sure that below it is the valley of the Sacramento River."

Back at the camp, the men were cheered. The end was in sight, and frozen feet and empty stomachs did not seem so bad. They went into the job of packing down the snow with new heart and new strength.

Through most of February, they inched their way ahead. Before they reached Kit's "little mountain" they had eaten the last of the nuts, and there were no more dried peas to make into soup. The men were forced to eat their dog and some of the mules. Only in that way could they have strength to beat a path for the other animals to follow through the snow.

At last came the wonderful day when the end of the snow was reached and they went down the last slope into the green valley. Food and rest and warm sunshine were ahead for men and animals. The work was done.

Fremont went on to so many long journeys that he was given the name of "The Pathfinder." When the maps were made, the entire face of America was known. Soon wagon wheels were packing hard the trails to the west.

Of all the land that was to become the fifty United States, only Alaska had unknown parts. Many years ago, Russian ships, commanded by an explorer named Bering, nosed into Alaskan bays. Captain Cook's sailing ships came there, too, just as they had gone to Hawaii.

Men rushed to Alaska in search of gold in the late 1800's. Many unexplored parts were searched then. In later years, hard trips like those of the early explorers were not needed. The click of a camera's shutter in an airplane makes a picture map that clears away the unknown.

The dreams of a Northwest Passage and a River Buenaventure are gone. In their place are dreams of what lies beyond the earth in outer space. Man goes on, drawn as always to explore the unknown.

CABEZA DEVACA

CORONADO

DESOTO & HIS MEN

CARTIER

CHAMPLAIN

HUDSON

LEWIS & CLARK

JED SMITH

FREMONT

Edith McCall, in her Frontiers of America books, writes in simple, uncluttered text without losing the dramatic impact of her true stories of real people.

Her purpose is to make these stories of our country available to younger readers and still vital and interesting to a wide age range.

Mrs. McCall now lives in the Ozarks and writes for children. For many years, she was a reading consultant in LaGrange, Illinois.